Harry

A Study of Teenage Mass Murderers

Harry
A Study of Teenage Mass Murderers

Cover photos copyright Neville Public Museum of Brown County

Second edition 2015
First edition 2014

Published by M&B Global Solutions Inc.
United States of America (USA)

Harry

A Study Of Teenage Mass Murderers

Steve Daniels

Harry

Dedication

This book is dedicated to my grandchildren,

Joshua, Isaac, Zooey and Penelope.

Hopefully you will be as proud of your papa as he is of you.

Harry

Contents

Harry

Preface

This is a book about a case that shook a small, Midwestern city to the core in an age of innocence. In the early1960s, Green Bay, Wisconsin, was a mid-sized city by population only. In reality, it was much smaller, with a quaint downtown surrounded by farm fields, open spaces and an American Indian reservation.

This is not an investigation into a who-done-it; but rather, a why-was-it-done? To this day, there remains no clear answer.

There is no question a teen-aged boy murdered his entire family and was arrested the following day. Yet this young man has never publicly addressed the reasons for the slaughter. If you are looking for a concrete, solid explanation of why, it will most likely elude you until the end of this book.

The killer highlighted here, Harry Hebard, is really only a masthead, a leaping-point to begin the real discussion. Hopefully he is the face you will come to know through the chapters. But he is far from the entire focus of this book.

Rather, these pages will hopefully serve as an overview of mass murder in Wisconsin, and the many men, young and old, black and white, who engage in this level of crime – a crime that consumes multiple victims in what is a single act of lethality.

As you will see, mass murder can be a crime of intent or of randomness. It can be premeditated or completely unplanned. It is victim-focused or an event of "Helter Skelter" proportion such as the Manson Family murders, killing whoever is nearby, a rampage, a killer run amok.

Along with the numerous faces on mass murder, you will be introduced to kids who kill. The reasons they engage in this most heinous behavior and its possible red flags will be addressed, along with the concept of active shooters and the school-shooter phenomenon. You will also become aware of the concept of serial murder and spree murder, two very different types of killings bracketed from mass murder.

Please read these pages with an open mind as you encounter the thoughts, ideas and facts to be presented. It might not help you understand Harry, but you will come to know mass murder – perhaps all too well.

Chapter 1

The Language of Murder

Harry Hebard's story is one of family mass murder, a multiple killing that turned a seemingly quiet house into a bloody abattoir. Yet in order to understand the magnitude of such an event, it is necessary to first become familiar with the language of murder. Grasping the totality of a killing requires students of homicide, professionals and casual readers alike to become aware of the various types of criminal murder.

In the jargon of crime, there are widely considered six types of homicide. These typologies, if you will, include single, double and triple murders, followed in scale by spree, serial and mass killings.

A single murder constitutes, as the name implies, one victim. This is certainly the most common type of homicide, often committed by someone close to the victim, such as a domestic incident where a husband kills his wife in the course of an argument.

Following suit is the double murder. This category describes two victims each killed in the same location, like a home, gas station or liquor store. In order for a murder to fit this typology, the victims must be found together, in close proximity, and whose deaths occurred from one event.

Similarly, the triple murder is contains three victims. Like the double murder, they must be found in the same location to fit this definition. Some criminologists argue three murders in one place qualifies as a mass killing, but conventional wisdom suggests it takes more victims to equate such a term.

The next three typologies are the kinds of killings that garner most of the media coverage. They are typically high-profile, headline-grabbing and always involve numerous victims across a diverse layout of corpses – a map of death. These are the types of murders that have been featured on television shows such as *Criminal Minds* or *Law & Order: Special Victims Unit*, as well as form the central plots for various mini-series.

The first of this group is a spree killing, a rampage of violence following the murderer or murderers across locations, venues and times. Spree killings include two or more victims in more than one location over what is usually a brief period of time.

These types of homicides are always part of a continuous, moving event of carnage, frequently including car-jackings, thefts, sexual assaults and high-intensity police manhunts. The perpetrators are in fugitive status, fully aware of the police presence amassed to capture them and filled with high-level offender excitation. In fact, the chase is often as thrilling as the actual killings to these marauding sociopaths.

The spree can last from hours to days, but is considered one continuous event. There is no "cooling off" period between crimes. Guns are statistically the weapon of choice for these predators, and their vehicle is an important tool, ratcheting up the spree's excitement. Driving fast to elude the authorities, music blaring, surviving on junk food, cigarettes and often illegal substances adds to the aura of the chase and stokes the fires of their psychological high. When two killers act in cohort, it appears they feed off the energy of each other almost like emotional vampires. The car is a moving abode for the killers, filled with the scraps and waste of the chase: old fast food wrappers, beer cans, half-smoked cigarette butts, dirty clothes and an arsenal of firepower.

Although some of these offenders die in a shootout with law enforcement, most are taken alive after the total exhaustion from the spree sets in. Some arresting officers claim to repeatedly notice a musky smell emanating from the captured fugitives. This could be from lack of personal hygiene during the chase period or an odor released from fear and elation.

Some call this serial murder at warp speed, or a moving mass murder. Examples of spree killings include Christopher Dorner, the rogue Los Angeles police officer who murdered three fellow officers plus a civilian, or the Beltline Snipers, who held the Washington, D.C., area in fear for ten days in 2001, shooting random civilians going about their daily routines.

Serial murder makes up the next category, and although there are multiple victims and locations in this classification, it is very different from the spree type. Serial killings likely are sexually based, fueled by the offender's uncontrollable, unstoppable fantasy of rape, torture and degradation. The killings can occur over a period of hours, months or even years, with each break in the homicides offering a cooling-off period.

Many killers, in an effort to re-live the rush of the murders, take "trophies" (often a body part), or "souvenirs" (an item belonging to the victim, i.e. earrings or necklaces). Although these items can satiate the fantasy for a time, this substitute eventually wears off, and the offender is driven to kill again.

Depending on which theory one follows, there are numerous sub-categories of serial killers. The classification developed by the FBI's Behavioral Science Unit is the most relied-upon and easiest to delineate. The bureau divides serial killers into three types: the disorganized, the organized and the mixed.

As the name suggests, the disorganized killer is disheveled, isolated, socially inept and has very little skill at planning the murder. His killings are usually a spontaneous blitz-attack using any available weapon. The offender does little to cover up his crime, and upon completion, returns to his residence; often a room in a parent's home decorated with items of personal fascination such as Nazi paraphernalia, *Playboy* pin-ups;, or to a messy, ill-kept hovel or rooming house. The disorganized killer has few, if any, friends, as well as a meager, poorly paid job. He regularly does not have a car, so lives in close proximity to the murder.

An example of a disorganized killer is Richard Chase, "The Sacramento Vampire." He was an emaciated loner who murdered six people in blitz-type attacks with little to no planning. He drank their blood, eviscerated the bodies, and took body parts as trophies.

The organized killer, on the other hand, is the polar opposite. He can be handsome, suave, well-spoken and present himself as a ladies man. He will have many friends, most likely a steady job and own a reliable vehicle. This type of murderer is meticulous in his crime planning, often stalking a select victim type. He will have a "murder kit" consisting of tools and implements to assist in carrying out carnage. These kits nearly always contain duct tape, rope, knives and masks, along with other items to overwhelm the victim, add to his pleasure, aid in his escape or hinder the investigation.

An organized killer can leave the victim posed for further denigration or will go to great lengths to conceal the corpse. They will also display certain post-killing behaviors, such as returning to the crime scene, incessantly following media reports of the crime, attending the funeral or trying to ingratiate into the investigation. Because of their stealth, this type of offender is the most difficult to apprehend. Ted Bundy is a notorious example of an organized killer. A handsome, educated law student, Bundy planned his attacks far in advance of the actual crimes he committed.

The mixed offender is a strange combination of the prior two categories, displaying some planning behavior yet showing a mess of instability and sloppiness. This offender picks and chooses – when he can – a "psychological stew" of mess and meticulousness. Often when there is a mixed crime scene, there are two offenders, each fitting different patterns.

In recent discussions among researchers and homicidologists, some are beginning to consider professional, hired killers, or "hit men," as a variance of serial killers. Their arguments could have some merit. However, in many of these hit men homicides, there appears to be lack of a sexual motivation or component. Rather, the murders are carried out for money, as part of an organized crime scheme to obliterate competition or means for groups to internally control wayward members. If a rifle or long gun is used, these killers are called snipers. But, as this sheds a negative connotation on the very same military specialty, they are now formally referred to as long distance serial killers (LDSK).

The final type of killing is the mass murder. According to many experts, there are five sub-types of mass murder: the disciple, the disgruntled employee, the pseudo commando, the set-and-run killer and the family annihilator. All five sub-types include a four-or-more-victim homicide in one location, resulting from one event. As of this writing, there has been a spate of these mass murders taking place across the country, each more horrific than the previous.

The disciple is an individual who blindly follows a leader, completely adhering to that person's bidding – including murder. These mass murders mostly occur in a cult-like setting with an extremely charismatic leader orchestrating atrocities. The Manson Family comes up as a prime example of this very group.

The disgruntled employee has, in his mind, endured a major slight on the job and must lash out in retaliation. The employee cannot tolerate being treated like chattel, and triggers range from being chastised by a supervisor to getting fired. The term "going postal" originates from this type of offender.

The pseudo commando is an individual caught in the paramilitary obsession. He is fascinated by weapons and has his own militant collection including military gear, manuals, training and maneuvers. He may attend gun shows, play paintball and subscribe to "Soldier of Fortune" type magazines, all in an effort to hone his skills. Then he chooses his victims, and in his mind, the killings become a martial engagement.

The set-and-run killer is a unique brand of multiple murderer. In essence, these individuals set plots into action and then intricately plan their means of escape. Unlike most other mass murderers, this person does not want to get caught. Julio Gonzalez, the perpetrator of the Happy Land Social Club fire in New York City in 1990, is an example of this type of criminal. Gonzalez was the jilted lover of one of the club's employees. After arguing with the woman and being thrown out of the club, he returned with some gasoline, poured a trail through the lone entrance and set it ablaze, killing eighty-seven patrons.

The killer in the 2007 Virginia Tech shooting encompassed aspects of a set-and-run mass murderer. He was disgruntled with his time at the college and felt he needed to act out violently against the student body. He additionally displayed characteristics of a pseudo-commando with a cache of high-powered weaponry, practicing the best methods to carry out his killing frenzy beforehand and to assist in his escape. He donned an all-black uniform prior to engaging in his personal "combat," and then recording the seemingly obligatory videotape rant or in some cases a rambling manifesto.

Last, but certainly not least, is the family annihilator, a term defining itself. This type of killer is often the "man of the house" who perceives something amiss in the family unit. These types of killings regularly begin as domestic disputes, exploding into the death of all present in the house and even others. With the deed complete, the killer typically ends his own life.

Understanding the concept of the bifurcated mass murder has risen to the surface of investigators' attention. This is due to the fact that a good amount of mass murders begin in one location and then move to another. For example, a killer murders his family, and then moves to his workplace or another location. There are now two crime scenes involved. The Sandy Hook school shooting is an example of this type of crime, in which Adam Lanza murdered his mother before heading to the school. Researchers have suggested replacing the spree-killing concept with this new idea.

Teen-murder expert Phil Chalmers, in his book "Inside The Mind of a Teen Killer," lists six types of teen murderers. The first and most commonly known is the school shooter. This individual carves his niche in history by attacking an educational institution, be it an elementary or high school. Often derived from bullying, this killer lashes out at those he feels have disrespected him in some way.

Often there are numerous victims outside these targeted bullies, and the abusers might not even be among the body count.

The next category Chalmers lists is the gang or cult killer. These kids use the energy of group think to act out their violent schemes. Relying on the urgings of existing group members, these youth engage in murder to attain status within that group.

Third is the crime killer. This teen commits homicide while partaking in another crime, typically offenses such as robbery, burglary or sexual assault.

The baby killer is the fourth type of teen murderer. Becoming pregnant as a teenage girl can be a terrifying incident. With the overwhelming idea of giving birth, telling parents or raising a baby, these teens panic and kill the newborn infant.

Next, Chalmers cites the thrill killer, someone who murders simply to feel the rush of adrenalin in taking another's life and the possibility of getting away with it.

The final classification of teen murderer is the family killer. In this subset, the killer is a juvenile who has had a confrontation with one or both parents. This teen feels slighted by these authority figures and finds his situation to be insurmountable, calling for drastic action. The killer often develops an elementary plan, puts it on paper and then determines a specific time to carry out that plan. A family gun is usually the weapon of choice, and when completed, the teen leaves the scene. In most cases, the youth is caught quickly. He has minimal resources to work with, as well as an ill-conceived plot from the beginning.

This exact scenario is the story of Harry Hebard. A young man who, for personal reasons, decided his family situation was so dysfunctional that five people needed to die. This book will delve into the events leading up to this young man's heinous act, its victims, possible reasoning and motives, as well as the psyche that made up the infamous Harry.

Chapter 2

Harry's Green Bay

In the early 1960s, Green Bay was a gritty, industrial city similar to other major rust-belt metropolitan areas. The papermaking plants were the major employers, hiring scores of men – and a few women – to produce the nation's napkins, toilet paper and tissues, while simultaneously befouling the air with a smell so rancid it could bring tears to the eyes. The city's only claim to fame was a National Football League team, the Packers, held over from the country's original town teams of the early part the century. The Packers were the dominant team of this era under legendary coach Vince Lombardi and future Hall of Fame quarterback Bart Starr.

Summer in this part of Northern Wisconsin could be hell-like. With no air conditioning and high humidity, some days felt so hot it was is as though Lucifer himself had unleashed the flames of Hades onto this municipality of 63,000, nestled on a bay of Lake Michigan. In the evening, people sat on porches and stoops, hoping some gust of breeze would attack the rivulets of sweat dripping from – and running into – every part of their body. With windows always open, couples could walk at night and never miss a play of the Milwaukee Braves baseball games wafting from radios.

At this juncture in history, Green Bay was virtually lily-white, a bucolic town peopled by European immigrants of all national stock: Poles, Belgians, Irish, Germans, Swiss and the like. The only minority groups of note were the Native Americans who had claimed the land for centuries, a few migrant workers and African-Americans, most of whom played for the Packers.

The city vacillated between rural and urban with a vibrant, old downtown district surrounded by vast expanses of farmland, worked primarily by the aforementioned ethnic groups. Many women were stay-at-home moms, opting not to enter the workforce outside the walls of the family abode. John Kennedy was president, and Roman Catholic was the major religious denomination in town.

Parochial education was in its heyday, with most religious-based grade schools overflowing. The nuns ran these schools with an iron fist, often rapping knuckles, pulling hair and verbally chastising those miscreants who failed to adhere to the dictates of Christian decorum. The Pledge of Allegiance was a daily event and Holy Mass was a must. Catholic boys were expected to act as Mass servers. Girls did not yet have this opportunity.

Public education in Green Bay consisted of a splattering of grade schools and three junior highs that channeled students into Green Bay East, Green Bay West or Green Bay Preble high schools. East and West were bitter rivals with little patience or taste for the other. In fact, the annual East-West football game often resulted in loud cross-town treks by unruly groups of students, minor instances of inter-school vandalism and even arrests. Students loved this weekend, parents tolerated it and police hated it. It was rumored that on one particularly violent game-day occasion, a squad car was burned.

Holidays were a time of glee. Halloween, often cold and drizzly, saw young kids racing home from school to make sure their costumes were laid out and ready to go. Suppers were gulped, homework hastily scribbled, and the long-anticipated ritual of putting on costumes ensued. There were no worries of tainted apples, poisoned candy or old, half-wrapped gum. Trick-or-treat festivities were always held in the dark, with as many kids and parents covering the sidewalks as fallen dry, crunchy leaves. Homes were decorated with carved pumpkins, lit to offer the utmost in creepy ambiance. Then, when the storming of local homes by scores of monsters, demons, cowboys, ballerinas and rag dolls came to an end, the urchins would run home, dump their loot on the living room floor, and count and gorge before bed.

Christmas season was even more exciting, usually beginning on Thanksgiving night with the unveiling of the local department store's windows. H.C. Prange Co., the owner of a Gotham-like, multi-storied major downtown Green Bay structure, started each season with three or four windows full of animated elves, reindeer, trains, toys and the jolly Clauses. It was a major holiday season event in Green Bay for generations. After a Thanksgiving meal of turkey and all the trimmings, citizens would line the sidewalks in the bitter cold to catch a glimpse of these windows. The following day, Christmas shopping began in earnest.

Shopping in downtown Green Bay was a slice of Americana. Seasonal decorations hung from the streetlights, music played outside, with records changed by a little old lady in an ice-cold booth. Throngs of people bustled from store to store, gleefully clutching their purchases and hoping for more. Snow covered the ground, and warm, coal-heated homes twinkled with Christmas trees and their multi-colored lights. The downtown scenes from the movie *It's a Wonderful Life* might as well have been shot in Green Bay.

The Green Bay Police Department was a mid-size agency attempting to keep modern, but facing a low crime rate. Crime, and particularly violent crime, was minimal in the area. Murder was almost a foreign term; intra-family violence and incest not discussed. Those ugly secrets were kept sacrosanct within the security of the home.

Patrol officers walked a designated beat, rattling doors and regularly checking in with headquarters on strategically located red call boxes. Drug use had not yet reached the area, and most police calls were due to bar patrons over-imbibing on a weekend night and then causing a ruckus. The police also dealt with burglaries, car thefts and other property crimes. In the end, if you had asked anyone in the squad, they would say it was a pretty safe town to raise a family.

In fact, prior to the Hebard family massacre, there was only one other murder with more than two victims on the city record: A paroled murderer named Thomas Ferry entered a local bar with a long gun and fatally shot his ex-girlfriend, the bartender and another patron. Then, while ratcheting another slug into the chamber, Ferry accidentally shot himself under the chin. Case closed.

After the Hebard family massacre, there was one more mass family killing in Green Bay, occurring June 15, 1999, in a quiet neighborhood on the city's near west side. According to Green Bay Police reports, officers were called to the home regarding a suspicious situation. En route to the scene, police were informed there were dead bodies in the home.

Ralph Farmster, on his way to work, had driven past his daughter's house. He was concerned because the windows and curtains were shut and he knew his daughter nearly always left them open. Filing this oddity in the back of his mind, he continued on to work. Upon arrival, he was informed that his son-in-law, Mark Grant, had not shown up for his job that day. Ralph left work and drove directly back to his daughter's home. Upon arrival, he found all windows and doors locked. He walked to the neighbor's home to borrow a ladder and screwdriver. After setting up, Ralph climbed the ladder, only to peer in the window and find them.

"Them" were his grandchildren, one-year-old Anne* two-month-old Isaac*. Once police arrived and entered the house, they discovered an adult woman, semi-nude and bound. The woman later would be identified as Farmster's daughter, Judy Grant, who appeared to have died by asphyxiation. Mark Grant's body was found in the family vehicle in the garage.

As a result of the investigation, police pieced together a logical scenario. During what appeared to be consensual adult activity, Mark bound his wife, Judy. Then in the course of this act, Judy allowed Mark to suffocate her (in today's parlance, this is called edge play). This activity went awry, and Judy died as an outcome.

In a panic and not knowing what to do, Mark made decisions with horrific consequences. Probably thinking he could not have the children live without a mother or with the shame of what he had done, he took the life of his daughter and son. Then, over what appears to be the next twenty-four hours, Mark engaged in numerous attempts to take his own life, finally deciding on carbon monoxide poisoning.

Although it sounds trite and rather passé, the 1960s really were simpler, more innocent times in Green Bay. Television was still mostly black and white, and many families still listened to radio dramas. Some of the top television shows were *The Andy Griffith Show*, *The Ed Sullivan Show*, *Ben Casey*, *The Flintstones* and *Gunsmoke*. There were only three national networks, and cable TV was years away from reality.

It was during these times that Harry Hebard was a teenager, growing up in a non-descript house on the city's west side, a semi-rural enclave consisting of tight-knit families. He lived with his father, Jack; his stepmother, Joyce; his stepbrother, John; and twin stepsisters, Janice and Judy.

The family included Jack Hebard, 37, (front right) and his wife, Joyce, 35; Joyce's 11-year-old twin daughters, Janice (far left) and Judy Rudell; Joyce's son, John Rudell, 15 (back left); and Harry Hebard, 16 (back right). Photo copyright Neville Public Museum of Brown County.

A home video proffered by the twins' best friend, Laurie Stelmach, shows two little girls who appear to love life. These fraternal twins loved to sing, ride their horse "Shorty" and engage in Girl Scout activities. Photos show them dressed alike, with shy smiles and involved in social events. Then, in a wisp, they were no longer in the picture, erased from the grade school landscape.

In contrast to summer, winter in Green Bay could be bleak and seemingly endless, with freezing cold bad enough to hurt. Dark, mushy snow from the occasional winter thaw lined the streets, and days that bled into early darkness, resting there until late the following morning. It was like this on the February day Harry carried out his massacre on Hazelwood Lane. He single-handedly ended the innocence and simplicity of this middle-sized city by the bay.

On this day, times changed.

Names have been changed to protect the dignity of the babies.

Chapter 3

The Fateful Day

On February 18, 1963, Lucifer laid an egg at 2626 Hazelwood Lane – and it hatched. Evil happened in the Hebard-Ruddell home. Sixteen-year-old Harry Hebard turned this suburban home into a blood-drenched slaughterhouse.

Harry was in the waning months of his junior year at Green Bay West High School when he unleashed his murderous fury. While in school, Harry was an active member of the track team, both in running events and pole vaulting, but was seemingly disinterested in other organized teams or subjects. He was a mere C student.

This apparent school-induced inertia did not carry over to his after-school time, however. In recent interviews, neighbors indicated Harry was very involved in setting up ragtag teams for pick-up games, enjoyed taking a leadership role in starting football and baseball games, and even laid out regulation-size ball fields for area kids to use. Although this young man appeared reticent to engage in long bouts of conversation, neighbors offered that he also was extremely shy and disliked being with others. Yet he clearly had a knack and a passion when it came to sports.

Dennis Carman, the self-titled best friend of Harry's step-brother, fifteen-year-old John Rudell, offers a picture of a peaceful time with Harry and John enjoying sports of all kinds. The summer days were filled with baseball played on a field carved out by Harry, who was known as "Butch." When not engaging in America's pastime, the friends played golf with clubs they manufactured on a course they developed. They had the most fun practicing pole vaulting and racing bikes on a self-made "hell drive stunt track." The pals would do bike stunts from track to track. Fall was a time for two-on-two football, again on a homemade field. Carman spent significant time in the Hebard home, often in the basement playing copious amounts of pool with John. By his estimation, they played about a thousand matches between 1961 and 1962.

Neighbors openly stated the Hebard household was "not a happy home." Those who socialized with the family stated there were often bruises on Joyce, and once, while at a group gathering, Jack twisted her arm behind her so hard she was grimacing. The look on his face dared anyone to intervene.

A close female friend of Joyce mentioned they would routinely spend time together talking, smoking and eating pickle sandwiches. During one of these talkfests near the holidays, Joyce whispered she bought a New Year's Eve dress, but "it was the last dress she would buy." After the murders took place, a co-worker indicated when he heard of the killings that he first thought Jack was the shooter. Another went so far as to offer the "house should have been burned the night of the murders."

Carman offers this insight into the home: "I did not like Jack, personally. He had an intimidating personality. My vision is that he never smiled. He wasn't vocal to anyone in the house, he was just there."

According to Carman, Jack could foster violence with the boys and Harry in particular. He offered this example. A school bully harassed and intimidated other boys, and must have challenged Harry. The bully came to the Hebard home to initiate a fight. It is unclear whether this bully brought other cohorts with him, but Harry's father came outside with him. A beating ensued, and although Harry's face was untouched, his hands were bloodied. Dennis said, "My thought at seeing that was this is not good. Jack has condoned a fistfight in which the other kid took a beating."

This was in direct contrast to what Jean Crooks, a cousin of Harry's who spent many summers at the home, had to say. According to her recollection, there was never any abuse she noticed.

The post-murder investigation revealed Joyce indeed made plans to escape the marriage, and mentioned she planned on taking her kids and moving out. In fact, one week prior to the killings, she visited her parents. Could Harry have overheard this conversation and attempted to intervene? A twisted way to keep the family together?

Many neighbors suggested Harry was definitely an abused child. His father, Jack, "abused him like hell," according to one neighbor who knew the family well. On one notable instance, Harry broke his arm and his parents refused to take him to the emergency room until long after the incident.

In another interesting twist on the concept of abuse, Jack was also an auto daredevil, calling himself "Lucky O'Hara." As Lucky, Jack was involved in auto tricks and was a human cannonball. Part of his act included lying on a coffin laced with dynamite near the lid. The TNT would explode, yet the daredevil would not be injured.

Newspaper articles had indicated Harry apparently hated everything about the thrill show, including the part where his father forced him to rebuild the coffin after each act. They noted Harry disliked the show to such an extreme that he never obtained a driver's license, nor did he drive any kind of car. In contrast, Carman offered that Harry had no such problem with the thrill show, adding he and Harry often rebuilt the flimsy, fake-bottomed coffins Jack used.

It appears this young man chose to lash out at what he considered abuse through petty crime. Harry engaged in house burglaries, stealing coin collections and other small items. Dennis Carman was the owner of the coin collection. Carman's mother found it missing, leading him on a personal quest to find the coins. Focusing on Harry, Carman went to the Hebard property in order to search for his collection. He looked in the trunk of a broken-down 1939 Ford, but he didn't see the coins hidden under some blankets. After the police were called in, Harry returned the coins to Carman. Oddly, there were no hard feelings, and the boys continued on as if nothing ever occurred.

On another occasion, Harry and Carman decided to walk the five miles to West High School in the middle of the night to steal a pole for their pole-vaulting exploits at home. Except for such petty crime, however, there were no real indications or warning signs for what was to transpire in this town, in this family, on that frightening day.

About a month before the murders, Harry, his stepbrother, John, and a mutual friend were involved in a shoplifting incident. This incident, combined with poor grades in school, a dysfunctional relationship with John, and some indications that Harry was going to run away, had his parents concerned. They took him to visit a local psychiatrist. According to court documents, Harry was found to have a personality disorder but was not psychotic. Another visit was scheduled, but the murders precluded this from happening.

Eerily, about two or three months prior to the killings, Carman had a dream that Harry was killing his family. This dream repeated itself for about four days and Carman thought no more of it. On the day of the murders, he didn't go over to the Hebard home as usual. Instead, he got off the bus and stood there awhile before walking home, arriving about the time his parents left for an outing.

It was dark when Carman attempted to phone John. There was no answer and he did not try again. He became so unnerved with the situation that he locked all the doors, turned off the lights, removed the pots and pans from a lower cupboard, and hid until his parents returned home. When he heard their car drive up, he quickly returned all the metal ware to the cupboard and greeted them as though nothing had happened.

On or around February 15, Harry attempted to purchase a pistol, but was informed he was too young. The following day, Harry went hunting using his father's rifles. This proves the boy was familiar with firearms prior to the incident and knew where to find them both inside the house and outside of it.

Then, on that day of uninhibited rage, Harry's plan began to unfold. This young killer attended school in the morning, but was absent the afternoon. With his lethal strategy mapped out, he gathered his arsenal and awaited the arrival of his many victims.

At 5:30 p.m. on the fateful day, Harry descended the stairs to the basement where the family guns were kept. He gathered his weaponry, a .22 handgun and a rifle of the same caliber. He then left the basement, exited the house through the back door, ran around outside and entered through the front. It was then he began the fusillade of bullets, unleashing a number of shots. Carman states that although he rarely went up to the room Harry and John shared, he did remember the rifle was kept in that room.

According to the coroner's report and case testimony, the first to die was Harry's father, Jack, from a bullet to the head as lay on the couch for a pre-dinner nap. Carman states that Jack napped before dinner, always. Anyone entering the back door could look into the living room and see Jack sleeping. Harry then fired two more pistol shots into his first victim.

A view of the Hebard house on the outskirts of Green Bay, Wisconsin. Harry ran around this side of the house, weapons in hand, before re-entering and going on his rampage.

Upon hearing the shots, John likely ran down the steps from his second floor bedroom. It would prove to be a fatal mistake. Seeing Harry with a handgun, John quickly turned to get away and was shot in the back. However, the first bullet did not cause enough harm to stop John in his tracks. He turned back to face his stepbrother and a struggle ensued. Harry got the better of John, pumping three more bullets into him, this time into John's head.

Harry then moved on and shot one of the twins, Judy, twice in the head while she lay near the icebox. Harry had now used up all the rounds in the handgun. Noticing it was empty, he dropped it, retrieved the rifle, and carried on to shoot the other young twin,

Janice. She had been coloring under the table and died after one bullet to the head.

At his juncture, Harry returned to the living room to make certain his father was dead. He grabbed the man's wrist, and after finding no pulse, returned to the kitchen to wait for his stepmother, Joyce, who was not yet home.

Joyce soon returned from the dentist and grocery shopping, totally unaware of the carnage in her home as well as the fate awaiting her: death at the hands of her stepson. Upon entering the home, she placed the bags on the dryer and stepped into the kitchen, where she stumbled across the scene of her son dead on the floor. With no time to react, Joyce dropped where she stood with one fatal shot to the head.

Harry checked Janice's pulse, just as he had done with Jack. Again detecting nothing, he moved upstairs, calmly changed into school clothes and returned to the downstairs area. Almost methodically, he checked the pulses of Judy and John. When he discovered them both still alive, he delivered one final bullet into each of them. Police reports indicate all murders happened within minutes, allotting little time for Harry to cool off and rethink what was happening. Then it was over. Minutes. Seconds. A blink. A blip on life's radar screen. Five lay dead, strewn about in a map of murder.

With hardly time for the acrid, thick gun smoke to clear, Harry changed, buried the blood-stained clothes he had been wearing and his weapons in the snow. As his plans indicated, Harry left the house with a bundle of clothes, met a friend at a prearranged time and place, and relayed he was running away from home. He spent that night at a friend's home in rural Pulaski, a small town northwest of Green Bay and only a thirty-minute drive from the site of the carnage.

The following day broke chilly and bleak. Darrold Aebesher, one of the Hebards' neighbors and Jack's co-worker, was on his way to work at the airport in the early morning hours. He drove past the

A police investigator displays the burnt food still on the stove the morning after the murders.

Hebard house and noticed the lights on, but saw no activity. He didn't think much of it until arriving for his shift, when he became aware that Jack Hebard was not yet in. Darrold called the Hebard home, but got no answer. He then called his wife to check if the lights were still on. They were. It was then he decided to call the police.

A patrol car arrived at 6:25 a.m. Officers, peering through the windows, noticed a body lying on the floor and immediately contacted detectives. The investigators not only found the previous evening's dinner burnt black on the stove, stuck to the pan, but five bloodied bodies. They quickly realized only one person was missing: Harry.

Harry's friend, Norb Hansen, displays the blood-stained clothes that Harry had buried in the snow in this Green Bay Police photo.

The morning after the murders, Carman walked to catch the school bus at the Hebard house as he always did. The other kids who took the bus were already there, gawking at the emergency vehicles. A girl said, "Something awful has happened there," Carman recalls. "My very instant thought was that Butch (Harry) killed the entire family, then committed suicide."

Focusing on Harry as a major suspect, detectives, led by Norman Daniels, began the manhunt for the missing youth. Green Bay Police issued an All Points Teletype to law enforcement agencies across Wisconsin. A short time later, an arrest warrant was issued for the apprehension of Harry Hebard, charging him with felonious intent to kill Jack Hebard.

While investigating the crime scene, Daniels and his fellow detectives found a note stuck in a pair of jeans indicating where Harry was headed. Detectives quickly learned a young adult friend of Harry's had picked him up and transported him to the rural Pulaski farm, Harry's chosen temporary hideout.

Police devised a plan to get young Harry into custody as quickly as possible. Because Pulaski was not within the jurisdiction of the Green Bay Police Department, they elicited the assistance of the Brown County Sheriff's Department. Lieutenant Richard Schrickel, along with another county officer and Harry's friend, who at this point still was unaware of the murders, drove to the farm in Harry's friend's car.

Seeing the car drive up, Harry exited the house and got in to talk with his friend. Lt. Schrickel, who was crouched behind the seat, immediately put Harry under arrest. Harry was charged with multiple counts of murder and was waived into adult jurisdiction the very same day.

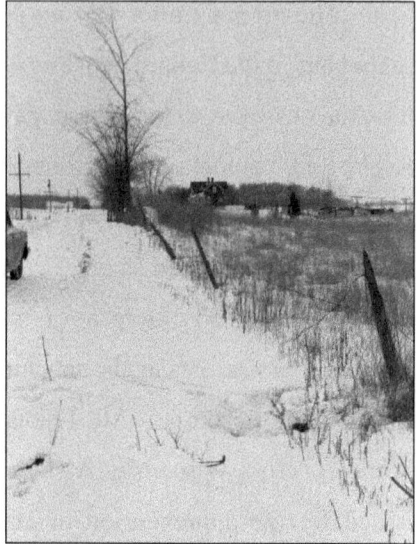

A police view of the distant Pienta farm in Oconto County, Harry's hideout following the murders.

The swift apprehension and charges were almost an anticlimax to a horrific event.

Soon after the murders, the Hebard-Ruddell family was laid to rest. Five caskets were placed in a horseshoe shape in the funeral home. Many persons, including the twins' classmates and Brownie troop, were in attendance. The classmates had created a huge memorial mural on the wall at their grade school. A friend of the twins reminisced how she found the arrangement of the caskets to be eerie and very sad.

A line of hearses transported the five caskets one hundred miles from Green Bay to the Central Wisconsin city of Mosinee for burial in the family plot. Hearses and cars strung out for miles along two-lane Highway 29, like a retreating army. Harry's cousin, Jean Crooks, recalled the line of entourage cars after the funeral service was the longest she had ever seen. Harry was offered the opportunity to attend the service, but declined; much to Jean's relief.

Shortly after the murders and events had calmed down, Carman walked to the empty lot about one hundred fifty yards behind the Hebard house, where all the pick-up sporting events had taken place. He stumbled across the stolen vaulting pole, which he broke into as many pieces as he could.

Harry

Chapter 4

Off the Streets

Immediately after his arrest, Harry was placed in the Brown County Jail to await the impending legal process. On February 20, 1963, Harry Raymond Hebard was arraigned in County Court Branch 2 on four counts of first-degree intentional murder. (One charge was held in abeyance for use later, if needed.) Harry was also waived into adult court, as his offenses were considered too severe for the juvenile system.

Only a few days later on February 25, Judge James Byers ordered the youth interviewed and assessed by two psychiatrists. These interviews took place over the course of the next few weeks, concluding on March 3, when Judge Byers read for the record the official psychiatric reports.

Harry's initial classification by the Department of Corrections noted: "The offenses were committed in a rather cool and detached manner," and "Regarding the offenses, precipitating factors seem to revolve around the fact that there were feelings of rejection and rivalry on Harry's part in the family and these feelings culminated in the offense."

Harry was found mentally incompetent to stand trial on the counts of murder. He was ordered remanded to the Central State Hospital for the Insane in Waupun for an indeterminate amount of time or until he could assist in his own defense. Harry remained in the custody of the state hospital until 1968, when he was deemed fit for trail.

On October 3, 1968, Harry stood trial in County Court Branch 2 before the Honorable Judge Robert Gollmar. (Incidentally, Gollmar also presided over Ed Gein's legal proceedings. Gein was the Wisconsin man whose grave robbing, necrophilia, murders and eviscerations inspired fictional movie characters including Norman Bates from "Psycho," Buffalo Bill from "The Silence of the Lambs," and Leather Face from "Texas Chainsaw Massacre.")

The jury found Harry guilty on all counts of murder. He was sentenced to life in prison, with penalties to be served concurrently. On October 4, 1968, Harry became an inmate in the Wisconsin State Prison System.

His life behind bars seems as bland as his life in the community prior to the murders. He has matriculated through all levels of security, from maximum (facilities with walls), to medium (with fences), to minimum (virtually no security at all). In fact, it is reported that he is an inmate driver, a position that allows him outside of the prison setting during working hours.

Due to paperwork issues and the miscalculation of some lifers' time structures, the Department of Corrections in 1992 mandated all inmates with a life sentence needed to return to a higher level of security until the documentation issue was resolved. Hence, Harry was sent to an institution with a higher-than-minimum security level. This was not, however, due to any behavioral problems on his part.

Program Review paperwork shows Harry displays excellent adjustment, allowing him placement in a less-secure level. He has held numerous job assignments within the institution structure and has offered no work-related problems.

Like most inmates, Harry has received a number of conduct reports. Living in a confined setting twenty-four hours a day with other violent offenders tends to lead to outbursts. He has spent time in segregation for fighting, and while in this status, has been issued other conduct reports for verbally acting out. No reports list the use of illegal substances or sexual misconduct. Neither have any attempted escapes occurred.

It appears Harry's conduct reports have tapered off as he has matured in age, as well as institutional existence. This has allowed him more freedom within the system. Because Harry has a life sentence, he does not have a mandatory release date. This, in essence, means he does not have to be released from prison.

However, due to the concurrent sentencing structure, Harry has been able to appear before the parole board on numerous occasions. Had the counts been consecutively, he might not yet be eligible for parole. The parole board continually compliments him on his progress while incarcerated, but always return to the issue of the seriousness of his crimes in their conclusions against release.

Suffice it to say, although Harry has been institutionalized since 1963, there is little of note in his record. He is a regular inmate, seeking freedom. He is no longer famous, and if released, most likely would not be recognized by anyone except his parole agent.

Local Media Coverage

The *Green Bay Press-Gazette* covered the Hebard case in detail. Below is a selection from two articles published in the February 19, 1963, evening edition, led by a three-deck, banner headline across the width of the front page:

Five Shot To Death on West Side

Harry Hebard, 16, Arrested After Family Is Wiped Out

Youth Caught on Farm Near Pulaski, Charged With Murder of Kin

By Bob Knaus

Press-Gazette Staff Writer

A 16-year-old West High School student was taken into custody at a farm in Oconto County late this morning about six hours after the bodies of five members of a Green Bay family were found shot to death in the blood-spattered far West Side home.

The youth, Harry Hebard, has been charged in the slaying of his father Jack Hebard, 37, his stepmother, Joyce Hebard, a stepbrother, John Rudell, 15, and his twin step-sisters, Janice and Judy Rudell, 11.

Captured About Noon

Young Hebard was taken into custody shortly before noon. After a search that began about 7 a.m. when the bodies were discovered. He was picked up in a barn on the John Pinta farm, located on Highway 32 several miles north of Pulaski in Oconto County.

A first degree murder warrant was issued late this morning, charging young Hebard with the murder of his father. The complaint was signed by Det. Norman Daniels, and the warrant, issued by Dist. Atty. Robert Warren, was signed by Judge James Byers, county count Branch 2.

Juvenile jurisdiction in the case was waived at the same time.

Object of Search

Young Hebard had been the object of a search since the bodies were found early this morning. Police said the two Hebard cars were found at home, one in a garage the other in the yard, indicating the boy had left home on foot. There also was a report the boy did not know how to drive.

He was returned to Green Bay about 12:15 p.m. and rushed into the office of Dist. Atty. Robert Warren. Warren refused to issue a statement immediately.

No details were immediately available on the boy's apprehension in Pulaski. Eight Brown County squad cars, the Pulaski Village marshal, and several city police officers were involved in the apprehension. Tear gas was taken to the scene, but it is not known if it was used.

The bodies were found about 7 a.m. today by two detectives who had been sent to investigate a report that the lights had been on all night and no activity had been noticed.

The report was made at 6:27 a.m. by Darrold Aebischer, a neighbor and co-worker of Hebard's at the airport. Aebischer had gone past the Hebard home on his way to work and had seen no sign of activity although the lights were on.

Patrol Car Sent

He called the home, but got no answer. Aebischer called his wife to check to see if the lights were still on. Then he called police to report something looked wrong. A patrol car was sent to the home and officers checked the windows. They called detectives when they found no activity. Detectives Dale Herfort and Robert Basche went to the home and knocked on the front door.

When they received no answer, they went to a rear door, glanced in and saw the bodies. The detectives forced open the door.

The bodies of Mrs. Hebard and the two children were found lying pools of blood inside the kitchen. Hebard's body was in the living room, lying on a davenport where he apparently had been sleeping.

Modestly Trim Home Scene of Grim Shooting on City's Southwest Side

By Charles House

Press-Gazette Staff Writer

The blood-red front door of the modestly trim white home in the southwestern section of Green Bay opened Tuesday on the most grimly shocking murder crime in the history of the city.

Lying in gore, five ashen-white bodies told the basics of the first chapter in the story of a crime which by noontime was winging its way across the world.

Dead was "Lucky O'Hara," the nom de plume of handsome Jack Hebard, and he lay on a divan in blood-soaked permanent sleep. Powder burns on his head were eloquent; there was a murderer who crept.

Dead also, and killed at shockingly close range in the small rooms were four other persons – Mrs. Hebard, yesterday a trim, pretty vital young woman; John Rudell, 15, her son by a former marriage; and a set of twins, Janice and Judy, Hebard, 11.

Absent from the white remodeled farm house was 16-year-old Harry Hebard. Absent, too, was a .22 caliber pistol, the property of the dead man.

"Young Harry is a moody kid," said a neighbor, "kind of quiet and sometimes in trouble with the police. He didn't get along very good with his brother, but he sure liked those little twins.

"The Hebards were nice folks, real nice, and I never heard of any real quarrels in the house except maybe between John and Harry, but it didn't ever seem as serious as this," he said.

The Hebard family lived quietly on about two acres of land on rural Hazelwood Lane. Hebard, always fond of cars and engines, supplemented his regular income by playing to county fairs in the Midwest.

"When I was a kid," he told this writer recently, "I kind of hooked up with a daredevil outfit, and I changed my name to Lucky O'Hara because I didn't want my mother to read that her son was in that kind of dangerous business. I always told her I worked as a mechanic."

One of Hebard's most dangerous stunts was to imprison himself in a breakaway box with dynamite. Clad in protective clothing and a helmet, Hebard would literally dynamite himself into near-insensibility and the breakaway box would smash from the explosion.

"I always loved the feeling of seeming to be reckless," Hebard had told the reporter, "and I like the excitement and the travel and I like the crowds, too."

Tuesday, the crowds gathered at the Hebard home, trim and white, with the blood-red front door – and it was not the kind of a crowd nor the reasons he would have preferred.

Chapter 5

Understanding the Killer

Psychological profiling (now called behavioral analysis) has been one of the tools used to confront aberrant behavior for many years. Forensic historians attribute its modest beginnings to Dr. Thomas Bond in 1888. He developed what many forensic professionals believe could be a rather accurate picture of the ever-infamous and elusive Jack the Ripper.

Dr. Bond based his theories on crime scene evidence; wound patterns and the skill level involved in the mutilation killings of Jack the Ripper's five female victims. He noticed a profile emerging from the specter of a multiple murderer, and a new branch of science was born. The following is Bond's profile as printed in "Naming Jack the Ripper":

"The murderer must have been a man of physical strength and great coolness and daring. There is no evidence that he had an accomplice. He must, in my opinion, be a man subject to periodical attacks of homicidal and erotic mania. The character of the mutilations indicates that the man may be in a condition sexually that may be called satyriasis. It is, of course, possible that the homicidal impulse may have developed from a revengeful or brooding condition of the mind, or that religious mania may have been the original disease, but I do not think either hypothesis is likely. The murderer in outward appearance is quite likely to be a quiet, inoffensive-looking man, probably middle-aged and neatly and respectfully dressed. I think he must be in the habit of wearing a cloak or a cape or he would hardly have escaped notice in the streets if the blood on his hands or clothes were visible.

"Assuming the murderer to be such a person I have described, he would probably be solitary and eccentric in his habits. Also he is most likely to be a man without regular occupation, but with some small pension or income. He is possibly living among respectable persons who have some knowledge of his character and habits, and who may have grounds for suspicion that he is not quite right in his mind at times. Such persons would probably be unwilling to communicate suspicions to police for fear of trouble or notoriety, whereas if there were a prospect of a reward, it might overcome their scruples."

Later, in 1902, German criminal police commandant Ernst Gennatt had the vision and foresight to develop a homicide squad, set the structure for murder investigations and employ early types of profiling. He is widely considered one of the earliest and most influential criminologists, and according to some researchers, he may in fact have coined the term "serial killer."

Inspector Gennatt was the lead investigator in numerous cases, including two infamous serial murderers: Fritz Haarmann and Peter Kurten. The Kurten case was featured in a classic foreign film, "M," starring Peter Lorre as the child killer. The lead detective in the film was thought to be modeled after Gennatt.

Just a few decades after, another type of profiling grew out of a need for World War II secret services to better know the enemy: Adolph Hitler. The Office of Special Services was charged with the task of developing a psychological profile of the dictator so Allied leaders could attempt to pre-determine his movements, interrupt the carrying out of his orders, provide a foundation to plot their counter-strategies, and make general determinations of how this dictator would react to military defeat. Ironically, the profile they developed suggested he would commit suicide if he felt his reign was crumbling.

After the war, Dr. James Brussel, a noted criminal psychiatrist, was called upon to offer profiling-type insight into many of the most high-profile cases of the times, including the Mad Bomber of New York City, the Boston Strangler, the Wylie-Hoffert "Career Girl Murders" in New York, and Dr. Carl Coppolino, a wife killer who used poison as his murder weapon.

The Mad Bomber

For sixteen years in the 1940s thru the 1950s, George Metesky, labeled the Mad Bomber, was a disgruntled public utilities worker who had been injured on the job. He set off over thirty bombs, wreaking havoc across New York City, but vowed to quit during the war. He planted explosive devices in bus terminals and libraries among other public venues. One of his favorite targets was movies theaters, where he would slice open seats, plant the device and wait for them to explode. Although twenty-two bombs exploded, no one was killed and fifteen persons were injured.

When Dr. Brussel profiled Metesky, he informed the authorities that the offender would be meticulous in his demeanor. He would be neat, tidy, precise and a loner. Metesky had sent letters taunting the police. Brussel figured that due to the style of writing, the offender had thought the letters out in a foreign tongue, and then translated them into English. He would be of Central European ethnicity and a Catholic. In fact, the profiler offered, when you catch him, he will be wearing a double-breasted suit, buttoned. When detectives located Metesky, he asked if he could "dress properly" prior to being brought in for questioning. He returned to the officers wearing a double-breasted suit. Buttoned.

The Boston Strangler

Albert DeSalvo was known as the Boston Strangler, the murderer of multiple women in Boston's Back neighborhood. In the early 1960s, the Boston area was in the grip of terror. Someone was sexually assaulting, strangling and leaving the victims nude in their homes. A Commission of Psychiatrists appointed by the Governor built a profile that was extremely accurate. The profile suggested the killer was thirty years old, neat, worked with his hands, and was either divorced or in a bad, sexless marriage. In fact, DeSalvo's sexual appetite was so voracious, his wife was terrified of him. But that same commission determined there were two "stranglers," while Dr. Brussel was the first to suggest the strangler was a single perpetrator.

The Wylie-Hoffert "Career Girl Murders"

Later, on August 28, 1963, the killing of two young career women brought Brussel into the forefront yet again when his profile helped apprehend and convict one offender while freeing another. The crime, labeled "The Career Girl Murders," occurred when two young women, Janice Wylie and Emily Hoffert, were killed in the apartment they shared on the Upper East Side of Manhattan.

Richard Robles, an admitted burglar, broke into the women's apartment and found Wylie nude in bed. He bound her, attacked her and attempted to sexually assault her. Upon returning home, Hoffert interrupted the carnage. She was also bound, and told the attacker she could and would inform the police. Fearing capture, Robles subsequently murdered both women. Brussel's criminologist experiences were chronicled in the book "Casebook of a Crime Psychiatrist." It is still considered a classic work to this day.

A Profile of Harry

In the mid-1970s, the Federal Bureau of Investigation developed a system for profiling those who perpetrate violent crimes, including serial and mass murder. Other professionals, schools and agencies followed suit, developing new and different methods that offered glimpses into the mind of a multiple murderer.

What follows is a detailed look into the psyche of Harry, a juvenile mass murderer, gleaning ideas from many schools of profiling thought. It will offer a portrait of this killer, an analysis of these murders, and a study in what turned out to be Harry Hebard's private day of doom.

What type of person is inclined to commit these types of killings? Some mass-murder experts suggest there are three categories of juvenile family killers.

The first is the severely abused. This is the youth pushed and punished far beyond the limits of normal discipline. Often times, this youth is singled out from other siblings and is emotionally, verbally, physically and even sexually abused by the father, with tacit approval by the mother or, on rare occasions, by an older, dominant brother. The abuse is so severe, the killer feels the only way to end the pain is to kill the torturer (as well as others that get in the way).

In one crime scene photo, Harry's murdered father is shown with his pants unzipped and his penis lying out in plain view. Although it appears this angle was never pursued by police or mental health professionals, this certainly might indicate some type of sexual abuse of the children. Interviewed neighbors said they would not be surprised if Jack Hebard had been sexually abusing the twin girls. Jack had been convicted of assaulting a woman in 1950, for which he was imprisoned. Neighborhood gossip told of Jack's voyeurism, peeking in neighbors' bedroom windows. Oddly, when confronted with this most bizarre crime scene photo, Harry indicated his father "always slept that way."

Dennis Carman, Harry and John's neighborhood friend, states Jack often slept on a daybed in the front room. He remembers walking past the sleeping figure and noticing his penis was out. It unnerved him so that he never walked past Jack when he was sleeping again.

But more than this, neighbors opined that Harry was, in fact, abused himself. They noted how Harry adored his dad, but was often rebuffed by the man. On a sadder note, Harry's birth mother treated him with disdain and a sense of callous regard. When Harry arrived to live with his father in La Crosse, Wisconsin, he was malnourished, dirty and suffered from enuresis (bed-wetting). On one occasion, Jack spent two hours on consecutive nights scrubbing the caked dirt from the boy's hands, knees and feet. Harry's feet were raw from the condition of his shoes.

The next category of killer is the extremely mentally ill. This child has lost all control of reality. They live in their own dark world of voices, demons and images, with a thought process so garbled it cannot be sorted out. In many instances, the child is deeply engaged in solitary activities that feed the confusion, such as heavy drug use, obsessive playing of violent video and role-playing games, and occasionally self-mutilation. This youth feels no one understands his personal pain and confusion, and there is no other choice but to kill.

This mass murderer is the most remorseful. Documentation and neighbors indicate that just prior to the murders, Harry was forced into a psychiatric visit by his family. Apparently, Harry was engaging in bed wetting, chronic masturbation and would hoard and hide underclothes in various locations. The attending psychiatrist reported he saw no red flags of a pending massacre during his one session with Harry, and a second session was scheduled for two days after the killings.

Carman attributed two other behaviors to Harry that, if accurate, were bizarre and worrisome. The family had two dogs, Curly and Pup. Pup was, in essence, John's dog. On one occasion, John showed Carman where Pup had been shot in the side, but she survived.

"It would not surprise me if Harry had shot the dog," Carman offered. "When I think about it, there was no one else around that would shoot a totally harmless and small dog."

Even stranger is an incident that occurred when Carman made his walk to the empty lot soon after the killings. The neighborhood was extremely rural, with only a small smattering of houses. Carman came upon a bushel basket full of human feces, which he believes had to be Harry's.

"There had to be something going on in that house in which he chose or was forced to do his business outside. I find it hard to imagine that he would have walked all the way to that spot to use the bushel basket."

The third and final category of a youthful mass killer is the anti-social individual. This is the type of case that garners much publicity, as the offender is killing for extremely selfish reasons such as money, freedom or a perceived slight from a parent or other authority figure. There is a plethora of cases across the United States reminiscent of this type of killer.

As in many other areas, Harry does not fit neatly into any of these categories. Rather, it appears from case particulars and mental health indices that Harry is a hybrid of all three: abused, mentally ill and anti-social. It has been documented he has remorse for the death of his father, yet voices ambivalence and almost relief toward the murders of the remainder of the family – even though his father remained the most important target.

Many experts suggest various types of mass murder serve two basic purposes. For example, felony-related multicide (the killing of numerous victims in the course of another crime) is instrumental for eliminating witnesses. Conversely, a family killing is an expressive act, highly emotional. One researcher states that in familicide "is not a means to an end, it is the end."

This is why such a large percentage of adult-family killers commit suicide. But, like Harry, most youthful family killers do not take their own lives. As with many youthful mass killers, he had a documented escape plan. Hence, he got rid of witnesses and eliminated his problem.

It should be noted Harry had two separate plans, one laying out a pre-killing checklist and the other determining the best mode of escaping and avoiding arrest.

Harry's Plans

Harry prepared his pre-killing checklist two weeks prior to the murders. Investigators found it Harry's English textbook in his school locker, No. 1295, during a search the morning after the murders. It is written below verbatim:

1. automatic .22 rifle and load it.
2. have feet wrapped in towels or rags.
3. hit Dad and Mom first, then as they come.
4. take all money & hide it in closed off chamber.
5. check everybody & make sure
6. get cleaned up & get into pajamas
7. get rid of towels or rags
8. walk around, in bare feet, to all bodies.
9. get shot in right arm & right leg
10. Call police or wait to get discovered. (1 or 2)?

Act through it several times & make sure you have it down pat.

Note this plan was somewhat detailed, albeit not very well thought out. He had items in the wrong order of importance, and some even contradicted others. For example, he was going to wrap his feet in towels, then clean up and go to bed, after which he would walk around the house.

Investigators found this next plan in a pair of Harry's trousers while searching the attic of the house. It is meager and does not seem to be well-focused; rather it seems hurried and lacks any detailed pre-killing thoughts.

    I.   <u>check list</u>

    II.   money

    III.   crap

    IV.   food

    V.   sleeping materials

    VI.   clothes

    VII.   weapons – ammunition

    VIII.   cigarettes

    IX.   school locker

    X.   materials to take with Pulaski boys

The second section of the plan is somewhat more detailed and goal-oriented, but immature in its lack of reality.

<u>Getaway</u>

1. Have back seat of Norbert's car completely empty. When I put all my stuff in it won't get mixed up with anything else. This will make for quicker loading and unloading.

2. Disconnect the phone as soon as Norbert comes.

3. If possible tell mom I'm going someplace so we'll have more time before realizing what's happening.
4. Having everything ready and waiting to be loaded. (go when Dad isn't home if possible.)
5. Lay up somewhere until I can take off from the farm.
6. Go to Pulaski high school? (if so, enroll by another name.)
7. If a change name have everyone call me by new name or at least a nickname (not Butch).
8. Have mail sent in care of Norbert

This plan offers at least some insight into his thought processes prior to the killings. It is evident they are the workings of an individual with limited resources and a teenager's imagination. Harry had some degree of organization, listing items needed. But his ideas in regard to avoiding detection were childish and indicated a naive rationale on escaping responsibilities.

It also displays how Harry, like most juvenile murderers, had no concept of criminal investigation techniques. The checklist of post-killing escape plans such as a pseudo-name and enrolling in a neighboring high school were simply silly, and could never come to fruition without at least an adult signature.

As a sixteen-year-old, Harry had no criminal sophistication. His dramatic thought process superseded any rational ideation. Harry was totally fixated on killing. Nothing else needed to be seriously considered. It seems after the murders, he assumed all else would simply fall into place. The thinking seems to indicate the logic of, "If I can kill five people, then I can surely avoid detection."

One area of Harry's existence that concerns this writer, but seems to have been glossed over in previous examinations, is Harry's chronic masturbation and hiding of undergarments. Teenage boys are normally sexually curious and often engage in self-stimulation, but chronic, incessant masturbation indicates something deeper and potentially darker. Couple this with hoarding underwear and the concept of the invasive sexual fantasy comes to the surface.

What was Harry fantasizing about? Could it have been violent, murderous daydreams, coupled with sex, that drove this youth to take up arms and turn lethal against his entire family? Without the ability to interview Harry, any ideas regarding his fantasy life are speculation at best.

When children kill their parents, it is called progeny mass murder. An offspring or adopted child, often for extremely trivial reasons, plots the killing event with mother and father as the main targets. Siblings are often an afterthought in the murderous scheme. This is certainly the case with Harry, as it appears he harbored no real issues with the other children in the household, save for his step-brother, John, who Harry outwardly envied for his good looks and easy manner with girls. Oftentimes, other children are killed by the lethal sibling for reasons such as not wanting to leave kids without a parent, a twisted type of family togetherness.

It appears the massacre of the Hebard-Rudell family by the sixteen-year-old Harry was the original progeny-mass murder in

Wisconsin. Research and news documentation does not offer any prior similar killings. It seems all familicides committed by a child follow the template inadvertently developed by Harry.

Researchers in the field of juvenile homicide offer the following ideas on progeny mass murder.

These individuals:

- Have a deep-seeded anger (Harry was rageful)
- Parents are the main target (father and stepmother, followed by step siblings)
- Usually don't get along with siblings (envious of step brother, John)
- Have some degree of mental illness (was seeing a psychiatrist)
- Have a high tendency toward sociopathy (lack of overall remorse)
- There may not be a precipitating event, and if there is, it is often exceptionally trivial
- After killing the family, there is a leaving of the area (fled to Pulaski)
- Unlike adult mass murderers, there is virtually no suicide among teens who kill

In Harry's pre-, as well as post-killing behaviors, there is documented evidence this was not simply a spur-of-the moment spasm of lethal violence. Rather, the events that took place were conceived in the mind of a rageful sixteen-year-old, fed up with his life within the confines of a mixed-family unit. Harry had written out plans to carry out the massacre and avoid detection.

However, following are the actions he actually took prior to, as well as on his predetermined day of the infamy:

Prior to the Killing
- Planned the killing for weeks
- Attempted to illegally purchase a firearm

Day of the Killing
- Rode the bus to school
- Feigned an illness at school in an effort to beat the family home
- Waited for each family member to come home

Post-Killing Behavior
- Felt the pulse of each victim to ascertain death
- Replaced one weapon in gun cabinet
- Changed clothes
- Took revolver with him
- Buried the blood-stained clothes, which were eventually recovered in another county
- Met a friend at a pre-arranged spot for transportation to safety

When studying Harry's thoughts and actions, it is easy to see a mixture of the childish and the adult. Certainly, this vacillation between simplicity and minor detail indicate this killer was, like many people his age, leaving childhood and sliding into early adulthood. Murder was his "celebration" of entry into manhood. This would be his ticket to freedom, his shedding the cloak of "kid's play" and blossoming into a new adult.

Richard Walter, the great American profiler, offers that for murderers, the act itself is a personal growth experience, a kind of catharsis. After the killing, the perpetrator moves on to a better station. Though perhaps miniscule, Harry fits this mindset, making plans to enter a different, maybe more friendly high school, change his name, and move on with life.

Chapter 6

The School Shooter

On Friday, December 14, 2012, one of the most heinous school shootings in American history occurred in Newtown, Connecticut. Twenty-year-old Adam Lanza, after killing his mother at home, forced his way into Sandy Hook Elementary School where he shot and killed twenty-six people, children and staff alike. Most of the victims were six or seven years old, shot multiple times with high-powered weapons.

An outraged nation demanded accountability, with law makers to mental health and school professionals waging a campaign against gun violence.

School shootings are not a new phenomenon. In fact, most people don't realize one of the earliest such crimes occurred on December 30, 1974, in rural Olean, New York. A seventeen-year-old boy named Anthony Barbaro plotted and carried out this school shooting, killing three and wounding eleven others. In his seminal work on school shooters, *Ceremonial Violence* author Jonathan Fast offers the following scenario:

"He [Barbaro] bought a 30.06 Remington rifle, at the same time began keeping a diary chronicling his plans for a rampage killing. He stored bomb-making materials in his room, including black powder, gasoline and tanks of acetylene. He somehow purchased a gas mask and hollow point bullets, items not available to the public. During Christmas break, he snuck into his high school and made a sniper's nest in a third-floor classroom. To the accompaniment of the Elton John song, *Ticking*, played on a portable tape machine, he opened fire from a window."

There were other shootings in the 1970s and 1980s. However, these school-focused rampages seemed to reach an apex in the late 1990s and disturbingly continued into the next decade.

School shootings, as evolved, can be defined as the discharging of weapons in, near or around a school with the intent of causing fear, physical mayhem or the death of persons associated with the school. In these instances, children shoot children, adults shoot students, and fellow students wreak havoc against their peers, teachers and administrators. Yet none seem as horrific as the events on that fateful day in Connecticut.

No town can be considered a safe haven from this type of carnage, but the town that spawned Harry in 1963 also gave birth to a well-planned school-shooting plot of epic proportions in 2006. Three students at Green Bay East High School, led by William

Cornell, developed a plan to "take out" as many fellow Red Devils as possible.

The plot failed when one of Cornell's minions informed another student. Once the plot was uncovered and police began to investigate, the severity and seriousness of their plan came to light. Police stated they fully believe the planned massacre would have become an actuality if not for the young persons who came forward.

This plot was so detailed that had authorities not interrupted it, the planned attack could have wreaked catastrophic casualties due to the planning of a trio of conspirators: Bradley Newtal, Shawn Sturtz and Cornell.

Newtal and Sturtz were rather non-descript – in fact, Department of Corrections Agent Bob Fusfeld labeled them "bumbling." They also lacked the desire to carry out the massacre. In contrast, Fusfeld said his interview with Cornell revealed him to be the "real deal," and an interesting person by his account. He was of partial Native American heritage, yet held an interest in the White Supremacy movement, or at least the trappings of the power that often accompanies it.

Cornell had what could be considered a shooting gallery in his basement, complete with mannequin heads that could have been used for target practice. He, like other school shooters, had a fascination with weaponry, and police seized boxes of guns, ammunition and homemade bombs from the two family residences.

Information gleaned from the criminal complaint and the *Green Bay Press-Gazette* indicate police seized the following items over the course of their investigation: an AKS assault rifle, sawed-off shotguns, a 40-caliber handgun, BB and pellet guns, along with other types of weaponry. Gas masks and walkie-talkies were located with two leather trench coats, gun and combat tactic magazines.

Authorities also recovered explosive-like devices. In searching the two homes, investigators found more than twenty bombs, consisting of BBs and gunpowder loaded into toilet paper cores, duct taped with firecracker fuses. Additionally, they found six-quart jars of homemade napalm, a substance that adheres to a surface as it burns.

There is evidence suggesting Cornell did detonate some of the homemade explosives. The young man had things so sophisticatedly planned that he possessed a map of the school, demographics of where various blind spots were, and even a plan to seal the students in the gym.

This offender was bored, probably had some form of depression and desired to make his mark. It was even rumored Cornell was partially motivated in his scheme to impress a girl with his prowess. Unlike many school shooters, though, he was not deemed mentally ill. He was most likely not a psychopath, but did enjoy the images of extreme violence. Fusfeld found Cornell to be bright, verbal, arrogant and even expressing a degree of empathy for those he thought were bullied at school.

This description appears counterintuitive, since many school shooters claim they themselves were bullied, ostracized and cut off from the mainstream student body. Luke Woodham (Mississippi),

Kip Kinkel (Oregon) and numerous other student killers felt so much peer animosity that they determined the only way out was to take matters into their own hands.

Many school shooters exhibit some signs of mental illness, but three alleged mass murderers in recent years leading up to this writing certainly could be labeled as seriously mentally ill: the attack on Arizona Congresswoman Gabrielle Giffords by Jared Loughner; the attack at the movie theatre in Aurora, Colorado, by James Holmes; and the aforementioned "slaughter of innocents" in Newtown, Connecticut, by Adam Lanza.

By all accounts, these three young men are poster children for the dangerously mentally ill, who are ubiquitously described as "falling through the cracks." Sadly, when they climb back up through those same cracks, they are armed with deadly weapons of mass casualties.

A small sample of school shooters not only wreaks their vengeance on classmates or unknown students, but on family members prior to the massacre, giving the aura of a combined mass/spree murder.

One such individual was Jeff Weise, a Native American teen who murdered his grandfather and his companion in Red Lake, Minnesota, prior to his rampage at the reservation school. (Native American is mentioned not to cast aspersions on this cultural group, but because it is an anomaly).

Over the years, numerous agencies have developed school-shooter profiles, most notably the United States Secret Service and the Federal Bureau of Investigation. In the September 1999 issue of the *FBI Law Enforcement Bulletin*, there is a multi-point checklist speaking on the profile of a school shooter.

Following is a somewhat altered version of that checklist. (The author has added ideas based on other sources and personal knowledge.)

Profile of a School Shooter

Shooters are overwhelmingly white males under the age of 18. There have been exceptions to the statistics, with some females involved in school shootings. Thirty-year-old Laurie Dann opened fire in a Winnetka, Illinois, elementary school, killing one and wounding two in 1988 before eventually killing herself. Brenda Spencer, age sixteen, shot at San Diego elementary school kids in 1979. She killed the school principal and janitor in addition to wounding eleven students. Spencer told a reporter she didn't like Mondays.

Some school shooters display both mass and spree traits. There usually are precipitating events prior to the shootings, and frequently these events lead to suicidal thoughts that escalate into homicidal ideation and eventual action.

A cadre of the culprits shoots family members prior to moving on the school. This could be for a myriad of reasons; however, intrafamily discourse is tantamount as an existing factor. A number have difficulty, or a perceived difficulty, with parents. Physical abuse, alcoholism and familial-mental health issues all could be suspect.

Shooters either obtain guns through legitimate channels or get them from a person they know.

Arkansas school shooters Mitchell Johnson and Andrew Golden obtained their weapons from a relative's collection, a storage room of guns that featured an arsenal of magnificent proportions. They allegedly pulled a school fire alarm and opened fire from nearby woods as students and teachers exited the school, killing four students and a teacher. Adam Lanza used his mother's weapons for the Newton, Connecticut, attack.

Many, if not all, had a history of mental health issues, and a few were in some form of treatment. Criminal justice professor Loren Evenrud, Ph.D., offers, "From a purely legal standpoint, it appears to me that the current crop of school shooters are deliberately indifferent to the danger that they are creating for unknown victims when shooting up a school with any firearm, certainly assault weapons! It is almost impossible for a layperson to determine if this deliberate indifference is due to an undiagnosed mental illness or a personality disorder. *(DSM - Diagnostic and Statistical Manual of Mental Disorders)* Certainly, these individuals lack any semblance of empathy, but it is not illegal to be emotionally vacant."

For many, violence in various forms plays an important part in their lives. This can include video games, participating in paintball, violent music genres or quasi-belief systems such as Goth, Satanism or white supremacy. A number of these individuals have a history of displaying anger or minor acting out in school settings.

For some, a special song or artist influences, but does not cause, the murderer to act. Others write brutal, violent essays for school, note their murderous thoughts in a diary, or focus on a special book, author or biblical sections to help fuel their motives. There is a true fascination with weapons, even practicing firing guns and setting off explosives. Military gear and clothing seem important to a select group. Some wear masks and many wear all black.

Many are loners, average-grade students who observers interestingly consider rather bright. Virtually all hate students they consider bullies, and some even show empathy for those who are preyed upon. Often, this dislike of select students focuses on those who are deemed popular.

Mass murderers in general – not just school shooters – express an interest in previous slaughters. They often display a desire to kill on a grander scale, to make their act bigger and better than the shooters before. Columbine, Colorado, killers Eric Harris and Dylan Klebold wanted to blow up the school and make it greater than the Oklahoma City bombing, somewhat like copycatting on steroids.

The majority of these shooters, and mass killers in general, feel a sense of overwhelming powerlessness. They decide that to kill is to gain back what has been lost and is rightfully theirs: self-respect.

There usually is no feeling of remorse after the killing is over. As a number of shooters end up dead themselves, there obviously can be no remorse. Narcissism, or a sense of righteous indignation, may attend to this.

School Shooters Contrasted and Compared to Harry

As the majority of this book is about mass murderers, a short comparison between Harry Hebard, in particular, and the aforementioned rampage killers is in order to assist with a sense of scope, scale and perspective.

The early family annihilators focused much of their rage on members of their immediate family or significant others. The school shooters usually bring that rage outside the home setting and into the school. Oddly, in most cases, these very places of the home and school are considered by most to be safe havens for youth. Only in the recent past have some school shooters begun to vent their rage by including parents in the kill.

In the 1960s period of Harry's mass murder, the weapons of choice were family guns, such as hunting rifles, small-caliber handguns and shotguns. Later, as the glut of school shootings came onto the American landscape, weapons became more powerful, lethal and readily accessible. Semi-automatic weapons have grown to be the guns of choice with their massive clips.

Harry's animosity toward his family had to be fueled without outside influence or inspiration. There were few, if any, documented cases of mass murder for him to relate to or attempt to eclipse. He was an enigma in his time. Unlike many school shooters, with their plethora of violent video games, video clips, movies and graphic novels to stoke the rage, Harry had a no blueprint set down by prior perpetrators.

The early family annihilators killed members of the same household, with victim counts usually numbering in the single digits; whereas the school rampage shooters could slaughter ten, twenty even thirty victims with relative ease. Teen family killers very rarely, if ever, commit suicide, while a high percentage of adult school shooters commit suicide or are shot by responding officers.

When comparing Harry to the modern-day school shooter, the scenario is somewhat different. Harry did have mental health issues and could not aid in his defense until he turned eighteen – five years after the shootings. There was discord in the Hebard family, and Harry was suspected to have been abused by his father. He has never publicly expressed remorse or sorrow for causing the deaths of his blended family.

Recall there are several types of mass murderers, from the para-military category to the set-and-run individual. School shooters fit into various types of these mass killers. Columbine's Harris and Klebold were very militaristic, while Arkansas' Johnson and Golden were-set-and-run types.

Fitting all violent offenders into a single, neat category can be difficult as well as limiting. Keeping an open mind hopefully will aid in preventing both types of tragedies.

Chapter 7

Harry's Legacy
of Multiple Murder

Mass murder in Wisconsin has a long and inglorious history. Victims have littered the landscape, stories have filled the newspapers, and killers languish in prisons for years, hopefully commensurate to their crimes. It is difficult to ascertain if Harry is the first actual teenage family killer in this state's history, but most research does indicate that he could quite easily be the first *documented* progeny family killer. He set the template for future juvenile family annihilators, offering a haphazard "how-to list" for wiping out a group of loved ones in one infamous moment of carnage.

This is evidenced by the fact that such killings were so rare that this particular massacre was covered by state, national and international media. If this had been a regular occurrence at the time, it is quite probable that it would not have generated such a reporting frenzy.

Harry Hebard was not the last mass murderer in this state's history, either. After him, they are legion, and the reasons, motives and excuses are as diverse and varied as the killers themselves. All are not family annihilation massacres or work place killings; rather, a conglomerate of drug/gang turf killings, retaliation slayings, race-based and even one without a clear motive.

One family mass murder occurred on the heels of Harry's case, carried out in Sheboygan County by a young man named Douglas Dean on a hot July 18, 1971. Either late at night or early in the morning, Dean consumed LSD, gathered his rifle and proceeded to shoot his mother, his girlfriend's mother and her three small brothers as they slept.

Dean, incensed at his girlfriend, determined that the ultimate punishment for her seeming transgressions was to kill all those close to her as well as the woman he despised the most, his mother. This case garnered much national publicity including a detailed, in-depth article in *Playboy* magazine.

Another case of a progeny mass murder occurred in the rural North Central Wisconsin village of Hamburg in Marathon County. This case changed the law in Wisconsin allowing juveniles, as young as fourteen, charged with murder to be waived into adult court.

On April 7, 1984, after a day of playing catch in the front yard of their home, the Reinke family was murdered by wayward fifteen-year-old son, S.R. Apparently without reason, this young man went to his room, removed his shotgun from the closet and the case, returned to the downstairs living room and opened fire. He killed his father, Peter; his mother, Caroline; his brother, Tim; and seriously wounded his younger sister, Christine, leaving her for dead. (Having failed in this murder attempt, the boy is a manqué, or someone who fails to attain a specific ambition.) Leaving his kin in what appeared a staged tableau of familial slaughter, this young man stole his father's truck and left the scene.

Due to the waiver law, this teen slayer spent less than four years in a juvenile facility for this heinous crime. Later, when as a young adult this killer re-entered the criminal justice system for another offense, he was asked by his parole agent what motivated him to kill his family. His only response was, "I decide when someone has to die."

It should be noted that these two cases, along with Harry's crime, were committed with the use of a long gun. This appears to be the weapon of availability, personal comfort, and choice of the early Wisconsin progeny mass murderers.

Other Wisconsin Cases

Ron Larson, of the Wisconsin Historical Society, developed a comprehensive list of multiple murders in the state since 1985, the first detailed study of this magnitude. This schemata of murder includes killings of more than two victims as part of one incident. However, from a previous chapter, recall that three killings are just that: three victims in one location. It is not considered a mass murder.

Following is a list of multiple murders in Wisconsin from 1985-2010. (Select incidents include expanded descriptions.)

1985

The Rev. John Rossiter, 64, and lay minister Ferdinand Roth Sr., 55, were shot in February while praying in St Patrick's Catholic Church in Onalaska. Custodian William Hames, 66, was slain in the basement. Brian Stanley pled guilty to the three killings.

1987

Four members of the Kunz family: Clarence, Irene, Marie and Randy are found shot to death execution-style in July in their dilapidated home in Central Wisconsin. A fifth member of the family, Helen, was missing from the home. Her decomposing body was found nine months later in a swampy area in the vicinity of the homestead.

The Kunzes were quite eccentric, living in the squalor of a home like something from a bad movie. The family was described as filthy, malodorous, and according to court testimony, relished in viewing video pornography and engaging in incest.

One young man, Chris Jacobs III, was brought to trial and found not guilty on five counts of PTAC-First Degree Intentional Murder. He was later convicted of kidnapping and false imprisonment in the disappearance of Helen Kunz.

1991

At Rama's Tap on Milwaukee's south side, three people were killed and another man wounded when opened a patron opened fire on New Year's Day. Police stated that a man in his forties was asked to leave after a dispute with a woman. He returned later in the morning, firing at bar patrons. The deceased were listed as Jim Guerro, 37; David Hamelin, 23; and Raymond Hernandez, 33.

1991

Rick Brenizer, 35, his wife Ruth, 31, and her children, Heidi, 10, and Mindy, 7, along with her child with Rick, Crystal, 5, were shot in May with a deer rifle. The victims were placed in the family station wagon, which was set on fire in a rural area near Balsam Lake in Polk County.

Bruce Brenizer, Rick's son, was convicted of the crimes and institutionalized under a unique sentencing structure. He would spend the first three life sentences in the state hospital, then would be transferred to the custody of the Department of Corrections.

1992

The bodies of LeRoy Weibel, his wife Ceil (both in their late fifties), and Suzette Frydenlund (in her late twenties) of Minneapolis, were found in the Weibels' mobile home in a trailer park beside U.S. 14-61 near La Crosse. They each had been bludgeoned to death with a blunt object. Suzette's husband, James Frydenlund, was found not guilty of the crimes. The case is considered closed.

1992

In December, three teenage girls and a boy were shot to death in Milwaukee in what is described as a vicious, execution-style killing of youths engaged with criminals. Each victim was shot five to eight times, and a fifth teen was found critically wounded after being shot and beaten.

Emmit White, along with his accomplices, Eddie Shumaker, Elliot House and Joseph Young, are all serving long sentences for the killings.

1996

On a cold, February day, four people were found dead in a northwest side Milwaukee suburb in what acquaintances speculate was a murder-suicide.

1997

Three people, two men and one woman, were shot to death in January and discovered by a teenager at a south side Milwaukee residence.

1998

Allen F. Krnak, 55, his wife, Donna, 51, and their son, Thomas, 21, are reported missing in July after their abandoned truck is found ninety miles from their rural Helenville home. They were scheduled to travel north to a cottage. Another son, Derek Anderson, who legally changed his name after the murders, was charged with the killings. The decomposing remains of his father were located in North Carolina.

1999

In April, three people were found shot to death in the basement of an apartment building on Milwaukee's north side.

2000

A fifteen-year-old boy was among three people who were found fatally shot to death inside a Milwaukee home in March. The two other victims were a twenty-seven-year-old Glendale man, and a thirty-seven-year-old Milwaukee native.

2001

Michael J. Wilcox, 49, shot himself to death in June after authorities searched for him in connection with the murders of three people: Joseph Hrpa, Robert Bowman, 53, and Gail Meidam, 39, in Townsend in Oconto County.

2002

William F. Reichert, 27, shot his wife, Miranda, as well as their two children, Cara and William, in their beds just prior to shooting himself in their Lincoln County home in November.

2003

Steven M. Tomporoski, 18, of Illinois, shot and killed his parents and an uncle at a family-owned farmhouse in Richland County in February.

2003

Jason C. McGuigan, 28, Dustin J. Wilson, 17, and Daniel R. Swanson 25, were found shot to death in June on the first floor of a Verona apartment they shared. Men Ju Wu is arrested and charged with the murders. He later commits suicide in jail.

2004

Six deer hunters were fatally shot and two others were seriously wounded by another deer hunter after he ordered them to leave a deer stand on private property in Sawyer County in November. Police arrested Chai Vang on the same day.

He eventually was charged with six counts of murder and convicted. He is serving his sentence in Iowa as part of a prisoner exchange in order to keep him safe.

2005

A Hillsboro assembly line worker, Joseph Gansert, 42, killed his wife, Mary, her fourteen-year-old son, and the couple's five-year-old daughter while they slept in their beds sometime during the night of February 1. The gunman then drove to his sister's home in Lafayette County, where he proceeded to fatally shoot himself.

2005

In what appears to be a gang-related shooting at a dice game, three individuals, Aaron Woods, Frank Mister and Ryan Lockridge, all 23, were shot and killed in Racine in July. Four other persons, a woman and three men, were also shot, but survived their injuries. Eight years later, Juwan Matthews and Demetrus Ozier were charged with the murders as a result of collaboration between Racine investigators and the work of a cold case review team run by the Wisconsin Association of Homicide Investigators. Matthews was in a California jail on federal drug distribution charges, while Ozier was arrested by U.S. Marshals in Memphis, Tennessee, as he tried to obtain fraudulent identification at the driver's license bureau.

2006

Terry Ratzman, opened fire during a March church service held at a Sheraton Hotel in Brookfield, killing seven and severely wounding four others. Ratzman was a regular attendee at these same services. Ratzman suffered from severe bouts of depression, was on the brink of losing his job, and allegedly was infuriated by a sermon given two weeks earlier by the minister.

2005

Amy DeBauche, 37, her father, David Jensen, 63, and mother, Jane, 60, all of Green Bay were shot to death in August. Amy's estranged husband, David DeBauche, was found guilty of all three homicides.

2006

Ambrosio Analco shot and killed Nicole Mariee McAffee, 17, her infant twin sons, Isaiah and Argenis, and her sister Ashley Huerta, 21, in June in Delavan before killing himself.

2007

Danyetta Lentz and her teenage children, Nicole, 17, and Scott, 14, were murdered in their mobile home on the outskirts of Janesville.

2007

Tyler Peterson, 20, an off-duty sheriff's deputy, went on a shooting rampage in October at a home in Crandon, killing seven young people who had gathered for pizzas and movies. A seventh person was critically wounded. Peterson left the scene and was later shot and killed by responding officers.

2008

Four people were killed at a Milwaukee street party on the Fourth of July. Antonio Williams had become embroiled in an argument, was subsequently beaten and had his watch stolen by members of a rival gang faction. Williams, James Washington, and a third accomplice, Rosario Fuentes, returned to the scene of the incident armed with SAK assault rifles.

The trio hid in a gangway between two houses, where they observed the block party in progress. They approached the house and opened fire on the gathered crowd.

2009

Three teens, Tiffany Pohlson, 17, Anthony Spigarelli, 18, and Bryan Mort, 19, all from Michigan, were shot in July while swimming in the Menominee River between Wisconsin and Michigan's Upper Peninsula. Scott J. Johnson, 38, was convicted of three counts in the sniper-lying-in-wait killings. All murders took place on the Wisconsin side of the river.

2009

A gunman opened fire in August on a group of people outside a trailer home in the Menomonie area in Western Wisconsin, killing three brothers, Toua Kong, 32, Siong Long, 25, and Seng Kong, 13.

2010

Christine Gollon, 30, and her two children, ages 3 and 2, were killed in their Nelsonville home in Portage County in April. The accused boyfriend, Shane Ketter, 36, was charged in the murders.

* This listing is courtesy of The Wisconsin Historical Society. Some cases were expanded upon and others were updated as information became available.

Every state has multiple murders, and as evidenced above, Wisconsin is not exempt from the carnage. The listing is certainly not all-inclusive, excluding multicides that readers have come to know as serial and spree killings. This chapter, this book, and the

Harry Hebard case are about one type of multiple-victim homicides: mass murder.

Harry's place is among this state's infamous. Harry could be considered a ground-breaker, a pioneer of sorts on the wilderness trail of mass murder. In 1963, he drew the psychological map that the plethora of progeny mass killers follow to this day.

Chapter 8

A Profiler's Perspective

Wisconsin is not the only state that has endured the wrath of teens killing their parents. Retired FBI profiler and Special Agent Larry Brubaker offers his ideas below on cases that happened in the neighboring state of Minnesota, showing how teen killers cross the lines of politics, families, towns and psychologies.

Kids Killing Parents

There are those teenagers who think they're smarter and more worldly than their parents. How many of us have fantasized at a young age just how easy life would be if our parents were dead, no longer around to tell us what to do? Many youths have had such thoughts pass through our heads, –but very few ever react to these ideas and carry them out. Such individuals only see the immediate future and never think about the ultimate consequences.

Psychologist Kathleen M. Heide wrote an article on September 1, 1992, in *Psychology Today* entitled "Why Kids Kill Parents." In her research, she stated there are three situations in which kids have been found to kill their parents, the first being the severely mentally-ill child. Secondly, Heide cites children who have been severely physically, verbally or psychological abused, pushed beyond their limits. Her third situation – and arguably the most controversial – is the dangerous, anti-social children, the darlings of the tabloids.

Severely mentally ill individuals are the rarest of these killers. These children have lost contact with reality and enter secure mental institutions rather than prisons. One such example includes a young man in Minnesota who cut off the head of his stepmother with an axe. He then put the head in the dishwasher and turned it on. His father was outside using his snow blower while this happened, completely unaware of the situation.

Afterward, the young man went out and told his father what he had done. The police were called to the scene, where they found the head well into the dishwasher cycle. The young man was soon shown to have a previous history of mental illness and is presently incarcerated at the Minnesota State Mental Hospital.

The severely abused child is one who acts out in desperation. Usually passive until the murder event, they feel they have no other choice but to take extreme action into their own hands. These individuals express sorrow for what they have done, but do not see themselves as criminals. Typically, their abuse is difficult to prove without independent testimony from other close individuals, such as family members or neighbors. Most of these cases do involve criminal charges and guilty pleas, but result in limited incarceration with extended probation and specific conditions.

The anti-social person receives the most publicity of the cases in the media. These individuals kill for selfish or apathetic reasons. Some think they will get life insurance payoffs and live happily ever after. Others believe that they will gain freedom and be able to do whatever they want. And still others have killed under the justification of dating someone their parents would not allow. Almost all of these individuals feel their parents are mean and not understanding of their wants and wishes.

The community of Rochester, Minnesota, experienced a very tragic event on February 18, 1988. Sixteen-year-old David Brom, a student at a private area high school, used an axe to murder all but one of his family members, an older brother who did not live in the house at the time. His mother and father were forty-one years old; his younger sister thirteen and his brother eleven.

Brom's killing spree occurred around 3 a.m. He went to school that morning and told a female friend that he could do anything he wanted because his parents were dead. He then went to his father's credit union and obtained $250. Later in the day, David went to another high school and met friends for lunch at a local pizza shop. He bought hair dye and returned to his house to dye his hair black. He called other friends and told one girl what he had done. He called the first girl he had seen that morning and she told him she knew what he had done. His response to her was simple: "I'm in deep trouble."

The Olmsted County Sheriff's Office responded to the Brom residence after receiving a call from a school administrator about rumors he had heard regarding David. Investigators found Brom's mother and sister dead in an upstairs hallway, his father kneeling half on his bed with the clock radio alarm playing. His brother was on his bed. The axe, covered with hair and blood, was discovered atop a pile of *National Geographic* magazines in the basement. The four clearly had been killed violently, their wound count a staggering fifty-six.

When investigators searched David's room, numerous items were revealed, some more alarming than others. His music choice was not extreme by any means. Artists like Pink Floyd, INXS, U2, Genesis and others made up the selection. However, in a notebook was written: (1) List: Food + drink + cabinet, stove, clothes, tapes - cards – game. (2) Cooler, *ice, Kill, bury, fast bank, Hair Dye (3) Bring tapes, beer – two or three cases, three cartons of cigarettes.

Lastly, on another piece of paper in his room, was "The Killings I'll do" and on that paper in red ink: "Will the Four Horsemen of the Apocalypse Ride...? Tonight..."

David was captured the following day when a citizen recognized him on the street and called the police. He was arrested without incident only thirty hours after the murders. David claimed his parents' expectations of him were too high. They made him do manual chores such as shoveling snow and chopping wood, as well as volunteered him to work for neighbors.

Interestingly, his older brother had difficulty with his parents as well, stemming from what was said to be tension over his strange behavior. He wore black eyeliner, jackboots and other unusual dress.

He also painted pictures on mutilated mannequins. David's brother eventually moved out after his parents became upset over a $65 library late charge for books on occultism, choosing to live with his girlfriend's family instead. He was only a sophomore in high school at the time.

David used his brother's move as part justification for his actions, arguing his parents treated him worse after his brother moved out. He told investigators that he wanted "to live as a person, not a slave."

He was convicted as an adult and remains incarcerated in Stillwater Prison, living out a life sentence without the possibility of parole.

The next parricide (killing of a parent) of interest took place on January 14, 2003, in the city of St. Cloud, Minnesota. Only a month from his eighteenth birthday, Jason MacLennan decided to kill his father. Jason's mother had recently passed away from cancer, and his father, Ken, had not remarried. The two of them moved to St. Cloud due to Ken's job, which involved frequent travel. Their home was in an upscale neighborhood, and Jason had the entire lower level to himself. This included a pool table, weights, a drum set, and apparently many other conveniences a young person could want.

On January 13, the day before the murder, Jason and some friends decided to skip school. When Ken returned later from a business trip, he discovered a half-empty beer bottle sitting behind the couch. Ken was upset, and made his feelings known to Jason.

Jason claimed his father was "belittling" him. His solution was convincing his seventeen-year-old friend, Matt Moeller, to assist him in murder. Matt quickly obtained a .22 rifle for Jason to use that night. The pair then devised a plan.

Just after midnight, Matt continuously rang the front doorbell until Ken awoke. When he descended from his upstairs bedroom to investigate, Jason opened fire. It appeared Jason hit him with at least one or more shots as he came down the stairs, yet still fired one round point-blank into his head.

Police responded to a 911 call from none other than Jason himself, trying to report the shooting. Upon arriving at the scene, investigators quickly determined Jason's account of finding his father dead was not credible. He and Matt were subsequently arrested for the murder.

Matt agreed to plead guilty and testify against Jason during his trial in Duluth in September 2003. Jason claimed his father was verbally abusive and distant. He even asserted his father had been physically once when he caught Jason smoking in the tenth grade.

Friends of Jason testified how he would joke about all the money he would inherit if his father was dead. Jason was convicted and appealed on the grounds of battered child syndrome, which refers to injuries sustained by a child as a result physical abuse, usually inflicted by an adult caregiver. The Minnesota Supreme Court affirmed his conviction on July 18, 2005, and Jason was incarcerated in Stillwater Prison, where he currently remains.

One of the most horrific killings occurred October 8, 2005, in Hastings, Minnesota. High school sweethearts Peter and Patricia Niedere were killed by their adopted son, Matt, and his friend Clayton Keister. Both were seventeen and seniors at a private, Christian school. The previous spring, the boys were in Las Vegas for school break when Matt mentioned to Clayton how much money he would have if his parents were dead. In September of that year, Matt told Clayton, "I'm really frustrated with my parents. I'm thinking about killing them." Clayton claimed that Matt threatened him if he did not assist.

They planned the killings during their high school physics class two weeks prior to the actual event. Another acquaintance, eighteen-year-old Jamie Patton, joined in the plot. Matt offered each of them $15,000 from the proceeds of the life insurance policy he hoped to receive.

On October 7, Clayton and Jamie were set to kill the Niederes in a staged robbery. Matt had given them a floor plan of the house, along with two shotguns, glasscutters, and a plunger to remove any cut glass. But when Clayton and Jamie approached the house from the backyard to the patio door, an alarm system tripped and lights went on. The two fled and called Matt, who was staying with other friends to establish an alibi. Matt urged the pair to return and complete the task. They refused. However, the ordeal did not stop there.

The next day, Matt and Clayton met around noon and went to Clayton's father's business, Gordy's Premium Auto Glass. Matt had a .22 caliber pistol Clayton had obtained earlier from the son of one of his neighbors. Clayton had a shotgun on him, and placed it in the trunk of Matt's car for temporary safekeeping. They then went in the business and had pizza with Matt's parents.

After eating, Clayton went out to the car and opened the trunk. He reportedly heard shooting soon after, followed by Patricia running over to him, asking what the matter was with her adopted son, Matt. She asked Clayton to call 911 and quickly returned to the store, where Clayton then heard more shots. Matt came out and told Clayton to go in the store and use the shotgun. Clayton did as he was told, heading inside and aiming his weapon at Patricia, who was trying to pull Peter to safety out a side door. His shot killed her instantly. Clayton would later claim he simply tried to, "shut my eyes and pull the trigger."

They left the area, with Clayton taking the two weapons back to his house for cleaning. He then cut the grass, showered and napped. He met back up with Matt around 5 p.m. in a northern suburb location, where they bought flowers for their dates to the homecoming dance that night.

After the shootings, Matt left his car at a grocery store near his house. He walked home and even spoke to a deputy who was watching the house due to the attempted crime the night before. He left in one of his parents' cars and went to the Mall of America, where he purchased clothes and a new cell phone.

The murders were discovered later that afternoon, and investigators soon believed Matt and a friend to be involved. The police attempted calls right away to Matt, but were unsuccessful in getting into contact, so they tried Clayton. When a Hastings Police detective called Clayton and asked him if he knew where Matt was, he told the detective that they were together, handing the phone right over to Matt. The detective then told Matt there had been an incident at his father's store. When Matt kept asking what happened, the detective – knowing the truth – responded by saying Matt already knew what had occurred. Matt responded with a simple "yeah," shortly admitting to the shooting during the same conversation, where he called his father "violent" and his mother a "bitch."

Matt and Clayton were subsequently arrested and charged with first degree murder during an attempted robbery. Both pled guilty with the possibility of parole after thirty years. Each blamed the other for carrying out the murders. Jamie Patton received a lesser sentence, since he was not present during the murders. All three are currently incarcerated.

Prosecutor James Backstrom told the media after the trial's sentencing stage that recent studies show the human brain is not fully developed until the mid-twenties. The last portion of the brain to reach maturity is the frontal lobe, which in part regulates aggression and impulse control. He said it helps explain why some youth seem to lack the reasoning ability to fully understand and consider the consequences of their behavior before acting. He added, however, that most teenagers understand the difference between right and wrong. "A sixteen- or seventeen-year-old of basic intelligence, who is not suffering from any serious mental illness or psychosis, knows it is wrong to kill another human being."

Yet parricide continues to occur, with about 225 fathers and mothers killed annually in the United States, less than the average in 1980s and 1990s estimated at roughly 300 per year. Statistically speaking, however, there are notorious patterns to these crimes. The majority of the offenders are eighteen or older, with males committing nearly 87 percent of the murders. The majority of the victims are Caucasian. Firearms are used more than any other weapon. Many perpetrators inform others of their plans, going so far as to involve informants in the actual event. Substance abuse does not seem to be a major factor with the offenders, and it appears conflict surpassed the offender's ability to cope or resolve any past issues. The rarest is a daughter who kills her mother.

What is the answer to prevent such events? There does not seem to be as easy solution. At the very least, parents should talk with their children and not just at them. Likewise, children should talk with their parents, attempting to engage in conversation and better understand the differences each has. Hopefully, this may be the start to reducing the number of parricide incidents.

Epilogue

Harry Hebard has been institutionalized since shortly after his infamous killings. Arrested within a few hours of slaying his family and placed in the Brown County Jail, he remained in this facility through the early stages of his competency hearings to determine whether he could assist in his own defense. When it was determined he could not, he was transferred to Winnebago State Hospital in Oshkosh, Wisconsin, where he remained until 1968. It was there doctors determined Harry was psychologically fit for trial.

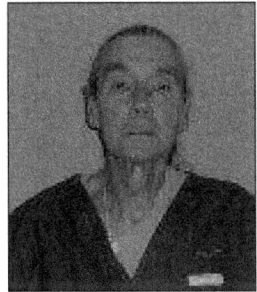

Harry Hebard's Department of Corrections photo, 2013.

He was found guilty of all five murders, sentenced to life in prison, and transferred to the custody of the Wisconsin Department of Corrections, where he remains at the time of this writing.

He has grown a ponytail to the middle of his back and now signs his correspondence as Hawk, which he contributes to an unsubstantiated percentage of Native American heritage. Harry has also expressed a desire to relocate to another area of the state, most likely to avoid the scrutiny in the eyes of Green Bay citizens. Coincidentally, he wants to reside at the same halfway house where the infamous Halloween Killer, Gerald Turner, confronted a staff member with a butcher knife and was sent back to prison.

Little does he realize that in these many years since the killings, he – as well as the city of Green Bay – has changed in outward appearance. Coupled with the fact he is no longer famous and many don't even recollect the crime, he could probably walk the city street without being noticed. However, if he is ever released, rest assured the Department of Corrections' parole agent assigned to monitor him will consider Harry to be extremely high profile, and due to being out of society for so long and possibly unable to cope, a high-risk repeat offender.

If Harry is ever released from the prison system, he will surely find himself in a state of re-entry shock. Since he has been institutionalized since 1963, he will have little concept of the world around him. So much has changed in more than five years that freedom could well be an alien planet for this offender.

A released Harry would encounter cell phones, iPads, personal computers, as well as a plethora of other electronic devices not around prior to his incarceration. Man has been on the moon, America has engaged in numerous wars, and the value of money has changed dramatically. Wages are higher, as are expenses. Needless to say, this man would have no idea how to function in a modern world outside the confines of an institution. He could not manage an apartment, pay bills or buy groceries. This, in and of itself, could present challenges he is unable to confront.

The House

The Hebard house on Hazelwood Lane has undergone many changes since the killings. Due to residential growth and a building boom in greater Green Bay, what were once vacant lots now make up a regular, bustling neighborhood. Also due to these many changes, the home's address was changed.

Sometime after the killings, realtor Jan Melberg moved into the house with no reported problems. However, later she sold the residence to Mike and Susan Schuster, who resided there from 1994 until 2003. Ms. Melberg informed this couple that murders had occurred in the property. Mike Schuster's aunt, who attended school with Harry, researched the case, ran off the articles and presented them to her nephew.

Susan Schuster, who considers herself an emotional person, located the spot in the house where each victim was killed. She stated she could feel where the mother had been shot while carrying in the groceries and saw where the father had laid dead on the couch. In fact, although additions had been made to the house, the original portion where the massacre occurred was still intact at the time. Susan even noticed the flooring behind the cupboards was there when the killings were carried out.

Susan went on to offer she felt the house was haunted and that some specter remained from the killings. Mike, who owns his own business and often had to work nights, would leave Susan in the house alone. On one occasion, she thought she heard a radio playing, but after a thorough search of the house, found none. The noise continued, sounding like an ongoing murmuring, a low, female sound that only occurred when Susan was home alone.

Ms. Schuster, who expresses a belief in some things paranormal, stated the sound was not frightening, but instead "soothing" and "not unwelcome." Susan talked to the "ghost" in calm and reassuring terms, stating things like, "So you're still here," or "I don't mind; it's okay."

At that time, Susan lived only five minutes from her work, allowing her to return home for lunch each day. Particularly in the winter, when the sun was shining through the French doors, she would sit in the family room and eat her lunch. While sitting alone, she noticed one blind would move back and forth, to and fro – but only one.

Thinking this odd, she searched for a draft, checked the fireplace, but found nothing. Every day while she was home for lunch, this "visitor" would come and join her. Sadly, according to Susan, all of the visits ended when the couple got a dog.

The Criminal Justice System

All of the individuals closely related to the case have passed away. Harry's defense attorney, Alexander Grant, became a judge and died many years later. The special prosecutor in the case, Donald Hanaway was elected state Attorney General, then judge. He died of cancer. The lead detective in the case, Norman Daniels, was promoted to the rank of captain, retired and died of emphysema. Even the police station, the sheriff's office and the county jail in use at the time of Harry's case have all relocated.

Harry has no known relatives and what can only be described as a minimal support system. If Harry should die prior to earning release, all that is left to mark his time on earth are scattered photographs, a fading mural on a grade school wall, and the graves of his victims.

A sad legacy by anyone's standards.

Harry

Questions for Discussion

1. After reading the book, what do you think drove Harry to kill his family?

2. In which category of teen mass murderer do you think Harry should be included?

3. Harry's sentences were concurrent, which means he could be released. Do you think the sentence was adequate? Was it fair? Should he be released?

4. If Wisconsin was a death penalty state, should he have received such a sentence, even as a juvenile?

5. If released, would it be okay if Harry lived in your neighborhood? Would you want to be notified by parole agents?

6. With the amount of violent video games, high-tech weapons and drugs available today, do you think Harry would be influenced by them? Would they have mattered in 1963, or was his mind set?

7. When you read the chapter on Harry's Legacy, which murders are triples? Mass? Attempted mass (called manques)? Not all murders in the chapter are the same. Can you find a common thread in any of them?

Harry

Acknowledgements

When writing a book, there are often so many people who influence the author's endeavor that it is impossible to list them all. Inevitably, there will be some deserving persons left out.

First is my late father, Norman Daniels, who retired from the Green Bay Police Department as Captain of Detectives, and who was the lead investigator in the very case this book is about. Often when working a homicide, he would be gone long hours from home, returning to take a shower, grab a quick bite and maybe a few hours' sleep.

When I was older, I would wait for him, sitting in the dark living room while he brought me up to speed on the latest investigation. These conversations piqued my interest in the criminal justice system, and violent crime in general. Yet sadly, I believe it was the stress of these same cases that led to his demise. With each new case his smoking increased, until finally he succumbed to emphysema.

Two very learned men in the field of crime influenced me in different stages of my life. Dr. David Walters, my criminology, penology and juvenile delinquency professor at the University of Wisconsin-Oshkosh, invited me into his world of crime. Dr. Walters was a Ph.D. who had been in prison. He made me think, inquire and dig deeper than I had before. As this was during the 1960s, the experience was even more remarkable due to the fact law enforcement-type classes were not in vogue.

The second figure is Richard Walter, a world-renowned scholar in the area of psychological profiling who mentored me in the study of murder. And what a ride it was! His style can be laconic, snippy and unsympathetic at times – but he really knows murder! To this day, I am in contact with him.

Additionally, I want to especially thank Bob Fusfeld, who allowed me to discuss my theories openly and aided with research into homicide, and Cathy Allcox and the Green Bay Police Department for the use of photos.

As for my friends, I can't say enough about them. What can be has already been attempted, often in the form of a joke, but always with care.

And it would be remiss if I didn't give a quick nod to all the murderers who were part of my life. As bizarre as that might sound, I spent most of my career with them and learned many things – some good, some evil, and always eye-opening.

Thanks to Mike Dauplaise, Bonnie Groessl and Amy Mrotek at M&B Global Solutions Inc., who lit the fire under me to move this project forward under my own power and not rely on others.

Lastly, to my wife, Nancy, and our two sons, Chris and Joe, who heard me talk of writing a book forever and never once doubted me. That is the best support a writer can get. I even told them on one occasion I would someday be on C-SPAN doing a book talk. It might not get that far, but hey, at least they can go to a bookstore or the internet and see the book is real.

To all of you, thanks from the bottom of my heart.

Steve

Harry

About the Author

Steve Daniels retired after twenty-six years in the criminal justice system, the last twelve as a high-risk parole agent working with extremely violent and dangerous offenders. During that career, Steve and a colleague interviewed and researched nearly two hundred murderers in an effort to develop a working profile for criminal justice professionals.

Currently, Steve is the chair of the Cold Case Review Team for the Wisconsin Association of Homicide Investigators, assisting agencies with old, unsolved homicides. He is also the author of numerous articles on various types of homicide, and is the coordinator of a nationally recognized annual homicide conference.

Steve resides in Green Bay, Wisconsin, with his wife, Nancy. He has two sons, Chris and Joe, and four grandchildren, Joshua, Isaac, Zooey and Penelope.

Harry